BASKETBALL
GIRLS ROCKING IT

BARRY MABLETON and ELIZABETH GETTELMAN

ROSEN
PUBLISHING

NEW YORK

Published in 2016 by The Rosen Publishing Group, Inc.
29 East 21st Street, New York, NY 10010

First Edition

Library of Congress Cataloging-in-Publication Data

Mableton, Barry.
 Basketball : girls rocking it / Barry Mableton and Elizabeth Gettelman. – First
Edition.
     pages cm. – (Title IX rocks! Play like a girl)
 Includes index.
 Audience: Grades: 7-12.
 ISBN 978-1-5081-7035-8 (Library bound)
 1. Basketball for girls–Juvenile literature. I. Gettelman, Elizabeth. II. Title.
 GV886.M3 2016
 796.32308352–dc23
                                    2015025145

Manufactured in China

CONTENTS

Y ou're on the court. The game is about to begin. You're face to face with the other team, standing on the half-court line. The referee tosses the ball straight up in the air. You and a player from the other team both jump, trying to tip the ball toward your teammates for possession. You're about to play an intense forty-minute match where you'll dribble, pass, and shoot. This is basketball.

In July 2013, ESPN published a report on the popularity of sports among teenagers. A study cited in the report found that 25 percent of all adolescent girls play basketball. That's the top enrollment for adolescent girls in any sport! One reason that basketball is so popular among girls is because it's one of the few sports that have been played by both sexes since almost the beginning. Basketball was invented by James Naismith, a Canadian-American physical education director, in December 1891. Naismith mixed elements from soccer, football, field hockey, and other sports. The sport was a success.

Just two years later, in 1893, a California teacher named Senda Berenson created a woman's version of the sport. Women at Smith College played against each other. By 1895, another PE teacher, Clara Baer, created rules of the game specifically for women. The sport became wildly popular.

The greatest triumph for women's sports would come nearly eighty years after the first game of women's

In an NCAA championship game, Lindsay Allen (#15) of the Notre Dame Fighting Irish moves toward the basket as opponent Kaleena Mosqueda-Lewis (#23) of the Connecticut Huskies defends.

basketball. On June 23, 1972, the Federal Education Amendments were signed into law. Of course, most people remember one specific clause: Title IX. Title IX gave girls and women equal access to sports. It states:

> No person in the United States shall, on the basis of sex, be excluded from participation in, or denied the benefits of, or be subjected to discrimination under any educational program or activity receiving federal aid.

It applies to all aspects of education, but its effect on athletics has been most significant.

Before Title IX, most schools had only a few women's sports programs or had limits on how many women could participate. Many schools did not have athletic programs for women at all. Title IX changed that. Basketball was already among the more popular sports for women, but since Title IX, its popularity has grown. Today, women's basketball has never been better or more prosperous.

Since 1997, there has been a professional league in the United States, the Women's National Basketball Association (WNBA), currently made up of twelve teams. College basketball is competitive and exciting at all levels—Divisions I, II, and III. In 1999, the Women's Basketball Hall of Fame opened in Knoxville, Tennessee. But most important, almost every elementary, middle, and high school nationwide has a girl's basketball team.

Both in and out of school, basketball is everywhere, and it can give you a lot of opportunities. Girls like you are out there on the blacktop—with each other and with the boys. They're playing basketball during recess, at lunchtime, after school, and on the weekends. They're playing with their friends, their family, and their classmates. They're playing for competition—on teams and in PE class—and they're playing to be healthy, to be strong, and to have fun. Sports let you sweat, run, play, laugh, and learn; they challenge your body and your mind. Girls like you are playing basketball because they love it. And every time a girl steps onto the court, she can feel proud knowing she's a part of Title IX, an important bill of rights for women.

Before you become a b-ball star, you'll need to know all the basics of the game. Where can you play? What gear do you need? What opportunities can the sport give you? For now, let's get you started on the basics. Who knows where basketball will take you?

CHAPTER ONE

GET ON THE COURT!

P laying basketball is simple. In fact, if you get creative, you can play it almost anywhere. To play basketball, all you need is a hoop, a ball, and a good pair of shoes. Even though basketball is a team game, anyone can practice shooting hoops by herself. In fact, you should start and finish each and every day with practice, practice, and more practice. That's the best way to become an expert on the court. Practice the basics, and with time, you will feel more and more comfortable playing and become a better and more confident player.

GEARING UP

Before you begin, make sure your clothes are comfortable. Loose-fitting shorts, a sports bra, and high-top sneakers will set you up for

THE RIGHT KICKS: CHUCK TAYLOR ALL-STARS

In 1908, a Massachusetts shoemaker named Marquis Mills Converse started the Converse Rubber Shoe Company. In 1917, the company designed the Converse All-Star, a lightweight basketball shoe with a simple, canvas-and-rubber design. The sneakers became ultra popular thanks to a basketball star of the time, Charles "Chuck" Taylor. The shoe itself even got the nickname "Chuck Taylors."

Often called "Chuck Taylors" after the basketball player who popularized them, Converse All-Stars were once iconic b-ball sneakers. Today, they're popular off the court as well.

In 1936, Chuck Taylors were the official shoe for Team USA in the first Olympic basketball championship. By the 1960s, Converse All-Stars were the shoe of choice for 90 percent of professional and college basketball players. However, in the 1970s, other popular sports brands such as Nike, Adidas, and Puma started designing better athletic shoes. Converse became increasingly associated with casual wear and counterculture. It no longer was the shoe most seen on National Basketball Association courts.

However, to this day, Converse All-Stars are a popular, lightweight choice for the casual basketball player and girls all over. They're a contemporary style icon and great for practicing. In 2003, Nike bought the Converse brand. In 2015, it introduced an improved model called the "Chuck Taylor II."

a practice session without any annoying rubbing and bouncing. It is much more fun to bounce the ball than to worry about your body bouncing all around as well.

As for the hoop, all you need is anything round—your laundry hamper, a hula hoop, even a spot on a wall above your head—to be a target to aim at as you practice your shooting form. Sporting goods stores often sell hoops that can be mounted on an outside wall of your house or more expensive hoops that are attached to poles. You might find a free hoop and a ball at a local YWCA, at your school, in parks, or at an after-school program. Plenty of public parks have basketball hoops you can practice with for free. Many cities offer

While any circular object can serve as a hoop, you should check out your city's resources to see where the nearest public basketball court is. There's bound to be one nearby.

free online guides to finding basketball courts in public parks, such as New York City's guide at http://www.nycgovparks.org/facilities /basketball or Chicago's at http://www.chicagoparkdistrict.com /facilities/basketball-courts-outdoor/.

Whether you're at a park or in your own backyard, you'll need to bring your own ball. You can ask for a basketball as a present at the holidays or for your birthday. You can also try asking your school if you can take one home some days—you can dribble all the way home! There are different sizes to choose from. There is a women's ball that is smaller than the standard men's basketball because women, on average, have smaller hands. There are also youth sizes that are even smaller. Once you're geared up and have a place to practice, you're ready to learn the game.

BASIC RULES

The rules of basketball are simple. The goal is to earn the most points before the game ends. The team with the most points wins. Points are scored by making baskets. Each team wants to make as many baskets as possible, while at the same time stopping the other team from scoring.

Basketball courts vary in size and surroundings. They can be indoors or outdoors, with hardwood or concrete floors. In middle and high school, courts are usually 84 feet (25.6 meters) long; in college and professional teams, they are 94 feet (28.65 m) long. The basket is 10 feet (3.05 m) above the ground, and the free throw line is 15 feet (4.57 m) away from the backboard, while the three-point arc is 19.75 feet (6.02 m) away for high school and even further for college and professional leagues.

A typical game lasts anywhere from twenty-four to forty minutes, depending on the level of play. Youth league games typically

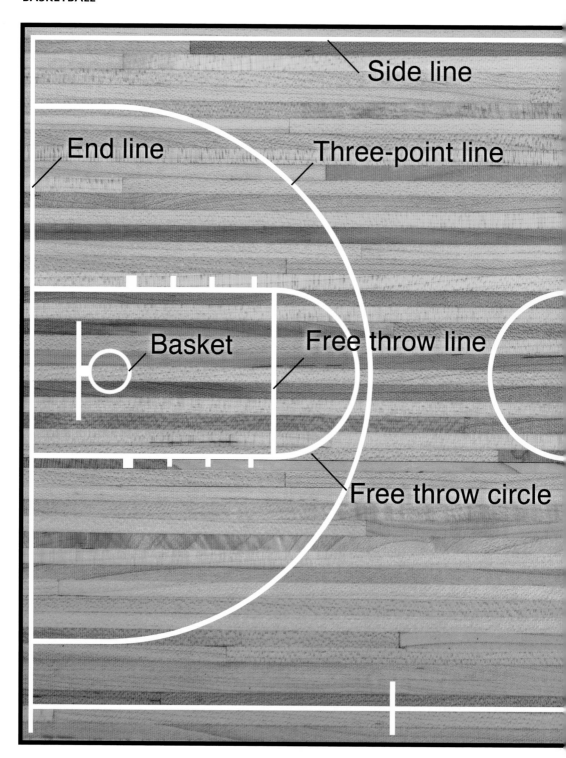

Side line

End line

Three-point line

Basket

Free throw line

Free throw circle

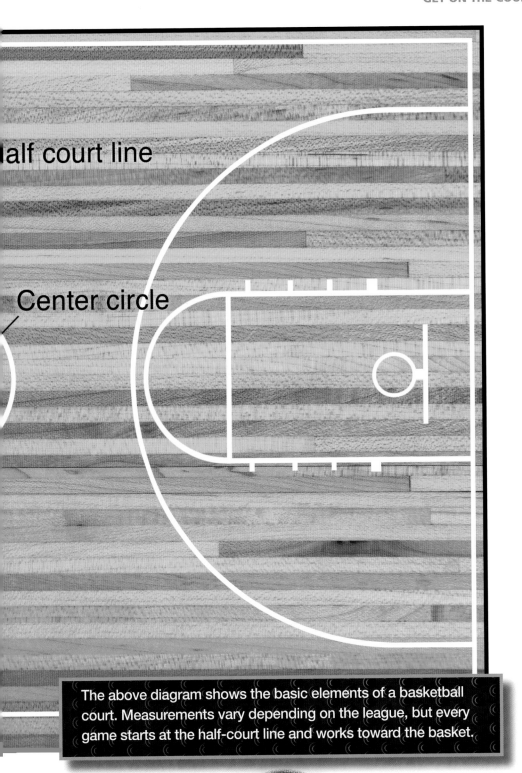

half court line

Center circle

The above diagram shows the basic elements of a basketball court. Measurements vary depending on the league, but every game starts at the half-court line and works toward the basket.

13

have four six-minute quarters. High school games are divided into four eight-minute quarters. In college, games consist of two twenty-minute halves. Professional leagues also usually play for forty minutes, but the game is divided into ten-minute quarters.

GAME PLAY

Every game begins with a jump ball at the center-court line. The team that gets the ball is on offense; the other team is on defense. The ball changes possession whenever a player makes a shot or when there is a turnover. A turnover is when the team on offense loses possession of the ball in any other way than a missed shot. No player can walk or run when she has the ball without dribbling it along with her at all times. That means she must constantly bounce the ball while moving. Once the player stops dribbling, she must also stop moving her feet.

Two points are scored for each basket made inside the three-point arc, three points beyond that, and one point each for free throws, which are shot after a foul. Each team defends its own basket.

A player with the ball can dribble, pass, or shoot. Each team has thirty seconds to try to score a basket. Passing to teammates allows you to then move toward the basket, cutting back and forth to get open—away from your defender—to receive a pass from your teammate.

RUNNING AFOUL

Moving with the ball without dribbling is a violation called traveling. After a violation, the other team is given the ball. Players unintentionally bump into each other on the court often; this is normal. But if a player violates rules in a way that causes significant contact,

Samarie Walker of the Kentucky Wildcats and Shanece McKinney of the LSU Tigers participate in a jump ball, each attempting to take possession of the ball for her team.

Oftentimes, a basketball player disagrees with the referee who has issued her a foul. A smart player keeps all discussion with the referee respectful, lest she be disqualified.

she'll be called with a personal foul. If a player grabs, holds, hits, or pushes another player or a referee, she is called with a flagrant foul. Any player fouled in the act of shooting gets to shoot two free throws.

Each player is allowed five fouls before being disqualified. After six team fouls—when the number of personal fouls of all the team members combined adds up to six—the player who was fouled last gets to shoot free throws, even if she wasn't fouled while shooting. If she makes the first one, she gets another. This is called one-and-one. When there are ten or more team fouls, the opponent who was fouled gets two free throws automatically.

A third type of fouls is called a technical foul. This type of foul can be called against a coach or the whole team for delay of game, too many time-outs, or too many players on the court. It can also be called for unsportsmanlike behavior or a violation of the rules of the game unrelated to contact with another player. If a technical foul is called, the opposing team gets two free throws and, in high school games, possession of the ball at the division line.

CHAPTER TWO

THERE'S NO "I" IN TEAM

Many sports enthusiasts get caught up in the game. Many basketball players feel pressure from coaches, parents, or peers to win every game. But the number one reason for playing any sport should be that it's fun. Yes, winning can be fun, too, but it is not the only reason to play. In fact, of all the useful skills that you'll learn in basketball, teamwork is one of the most important. Being able to communicate and cooperate with a group of people is an essential part of most jobs. People who work well on teams succeed—that's a fact! So let's learn about teamwork.

WHO'S ON THE TEAM?

A standard basketball team consists of twelve players, plus the coaches. There may be one, two, or even three coaches. Ten players

The Maryland Terrapins huddle to discuss strategy before a game against the Michigan State Spartans. Teamwork is key to winning a basketball game.

MAKINGS OF A STAR: MAYA MOORE

Women's basketball has grown significantly since the formation of the WNBA in 1996. Today, the women's league is formed of over 140 of the best women basketball players. These talented athletes are part of a new generation of role models for all women who love sports—basketball or otherwise.

Born in 1989, Maya Moore was just eight years old when the first WNBA game was played in 1997. In both 2006 and 2007, she won the Naismith Prep Player of the Year award, awarded to the top male and female high school basketball player each year. Then, in 2009 and 2010, she led her team at the University of Connecticut to back-to-back national championships and a record-setting ninety wins in a row. In 2011, she was the top pick in the WNBA draft, joining the Minnesota Lynx.

Since joining the Minnesota Lynx, Moore's only gone on to bigger and better wins. Off-season, she has played on international teams in Spain and China—leading the latter to its first-ever championship title. In 2012, she was part of Team USA at the Olympics, winning gold. In later WNBA seasons, she continued to be a force to be reckoned with and made headlines with her record-setting shots. In 2014, she won the WNBA Most Valuable Player Award.

So what makes Maya such an incredible forward? In a June 2015 interview with Sporting News, Moore had the following to say:

I've had great coaches and teachers of the game help me appreciate and try to challenge myself in different areas of the games. Using statistics. Trying to be efficient. So I've looked at my stats since a young age and tried to understand the benefit of using statistics to be efficient but at the same time not being too consumed with it and trying to just play, get a feel when I'm out there on the court, trusting my instincts.

Maya Moore of the Minnesota Lynx is possibly the most notable WNBA star of our time thanks to her superior skills on the court.

Moore's self-awareness and discipline are essential. They've helped her perfect her skills on the court and continually get better. It would be easy to achieve success and stop training, practicing, or looking for areas of improvement. But Maya Moore stays humble, always pushing her own limits and inspiring young female basketball players the world over.

encouragement to their team. However, it is never appropriate to jeer at the opposing team or boo.

The five players on the court are two guards, two forwards, and one center. The guards are usually the best ball handlers. They advance the ball up the court by dribbling and passing. The point guard is the floor leader—she dribbles the ball up the court and calls a play for the team to run. Usually the point guard is a fast, smaller player with great ball-handling skills. She has the ball more than any other player, although her job is to pass it to others who do more of the scoring.

The second guard, also known as the shooting guard, is a quick, accurate long-range shot. The next player is the small forward, usually taller than the guards, with an accurate outside shot and the ability to go inside and rebound. Inside, with their backs to the basket, are the other forward and the center. This second forward is the power forward. She starts from the block and posts up inside to make powerful moves to score baskets, rebound, or set screens. The center, the fifth player, is usually the tallest player on the team. She jumps center at the beginning of the game, posts up on the block, and works to block other players' shots on defense.

One of the best things about basketball is that it's a team sport. These five players work together toward a common goal. No matter how great one player is, it would be incredibly difficult to move across the court without relying on her teammates. Learning to work as a team is a skill that any woman will need in life and on the job. Good teamwork will always bring success—in any field.

KEEP IT UP OFF-SEASON

At the end of the season, only one team in any given league ends with a win. However, that does not have to mean that the season was a loss. If you can let the game become more a way of living—of dedicating yourself to something that pushes your limits, physically and mentally, and bonds you with other people—then you can feel good about any game or season, win or lose.

Once you get involved in a school team, you will play throughout the season, usually during the winter months. During the summer, you can attend one of the many sport camps in the United States and Canada. You can search online for sports camps in your area, or contact local colleges and ask if they host a girls' basketball camp in the summer. You can even meet up with your regular teammates. All those hours practicing and traveling to games year-round are bound to make you and your teammates close. It's natural that in the summer, you'll want to keep up that friendship. Plus, the summer is a great time to improve your skills and to work on the parts of your game that you don't feel confident about in league games.

CHAPTER THREE

BALL HANDLING, DEFENSE, AND PASSING

Every game of basketball involves certain skills. For now, we'll cover some of the essentials. Ball handling is important, as it forms the basis of the game. The ability to control the ball and move across the court keeps the game going. Passing is also important, as it promotes teamwork and will often rescue a player from a dire situation. We'll also discuss defense: how to keep the other team from scoring baskets.

These skills all rely on speed, agility, and great footwork. Every basketball star spends hundreds of hours working on her dribble and defensive stance. Don't worry if these skills seem confusing. Let's break down each one so we can better understand the game. Then later we can get into shooting and rebounding.

MAKE A ROUTINE AND STICK TO IT!

One skill that basketball will help you develop is discipline. This will help you greatly both on and off the court. Discipline—having the self-control to create a routine and stick to it—is important in school, work, and all sorts of hobbies. It's particularly key to diet and exercise. Make a training routine to perfect your on-court skills. If you do so, you'll be a star player in no time.

Because a basketball game requires you to use your whole body, you must get ready first by stretching thoroughly before and

Make stretching a regular part of your pre-game routine. It will help your body prepare for strenuous activity on the court, as well as prevent injuries from pulled muscles.

after practices and games. Work to develop your muscles, which will help you improve your skills with the ball. Train both with the ball and without it. Spend equal time on each if you can. If you don't have enough time in one day, then be sure to split up the drills so that you cover different skills on different days. For example, if you cover shooting and defense one day, then you should practice passing and ball handling the next. Your average training day should be forty-five minutes to an hour and a half. It should include:

- Five minutes of warm-up: Jog around the playground or around the block.
- Ten minutes of stretching: Always stretch after you get warm; this way your muscles will be warm and you can avoid injury.
- Five minutes of footwork and agility games.
- Five to ten minutes each of ball handling, rebounding, shooting, and passing games (maybe two one day and two the next).
- Five minutes of defensive slides.
- Five minutes of cool down and stretching.

BALL HANDLING

You dribble to advance the ball up the court when there is no one open to pass to or when you are not open to shoot. The more comfortable you are with the ball in your hands under any conditions, the more successful a ball handler you will be. You want to work every day to become a better ball handler and a better dribbler.

There are several types of dribbles: the crossover, between the legs, behind-the-back, spin, and speed. The more you practice all of these, the more natural they will feel. You want the ball to feel like an extension of your hand.

NUTRITION AND HEALTH

A lot of middle school and high school students feel like they have low energy all the time. "Why?" you might wonder. Some teenagers seem like they are barely able to make it through the day. A lot of this has to do with diet.

If you eat junk food, unhealthy snacks, and sugary drinks, your energy levels are going to be much lower than if you have a healthy, balanced diet. Junk food will not fuel you through the day. There are simple solutions to eating healthy. Try bringing some leftovers from last night's dinner to have for lunch at school. Eat more vegetables and pastas. You can still have potato chips and soda every once in awhile, but balance it out with healthy

Physical exercise and proper nutrition go hand-in-hand when it comes to good health. Fresh fruits and veggies make a great courtside snack. Avoid junk food.

(continued on the next page)

(continued from the previous page)

choices. Soon, you'll be the leading scorer in your league.

Taking care of your body should be a daily practice. Eat right and stay away from alcohol and drugs. In no time, you'll be the envy of other players as you effortlessly dribble across the court.

Three skills to remember for ball handling are:

- Dribble with your finger pads (from your fingertips down to the first joint).
- Dribble low (below your bent knees).
- Keep your eyes up and look down the court.

Following are some games you can play to practice your handling of the ball.

Fingertips

Stretch your arms in front of you, palms up. Toss the ball from your left to your right hand using only the pads of your fingers. Next, move your hands down to knee level and do it again.

Pound the Ground

Dribble with your right hand fifty times as fast as you can, keeping the ball close to the ground. Repeat with the left hand. Next, do fifty dribbles passing the ball back and forth from your left to right hand. Work your way up to more dribbles for each exercise.

Chakecia Miller of the George Washington Colonials dribbles the basketball up the court during a game. Expert ball handling is crucial to winning the game.

Full Court Dribble

Dribble down the court with your right hand. Turn around and dribble back with your left. Try it walking once, then jogging, then running, and finally sprinting. Be sure to control your dribble and keep your eyes up.

Crossover

Dribble up the court, making three dribbles to the left, then cross over with one low dribble to change directions, then make three dribbles to the right. Repeat all the way down the court and back.

Between the Legs

Same as above, but this time change directions by dribbling between your legs.

Behind the Back

Same as above, this time changing directions with one hard dribble behind your back.

Spin Move

Cup the ball in your arm and pivot backward and around swinging the ball back.

Once you practice each dribble separately, you can combine these moves as you dribble up and down the court.

DEFENSE

A well-known basketball saying goes, "Offense sells tickets, defense wins games." It is true that the excitement of the game—the scoring and highlights—come on the offensive end, when your team has the opportunity to score. However, good defense is the key to a team's success, and also to an individual's success as an all-around player. Defense is not only a skill; it's also a measure of determination. If you practice your footwork and focus on stopping your opponent, you will be a good defender and incredibly valuable to any team.

The point of defense is to stop the offense from scoring. This is done by stealing the ball (a pass or a dribble), rebounding a missed shot, or forcing a turnover—so that the other team does not get a shot off in thirty seconds or so that any shot taken is poor and doesn't go in. Defense is played either person-to-person, where you face up and play defense against one player wherever she goes on the court, or it is played in a zone, where defenders cover a designated area of the court and guard whichever player is in their area at that time. There are three skills to remember for defense:

- Stay low and keep your hands up. (Bend your knees, bringing your thighs almost parallel to the ground.)
- Slide your feet, but don't touch your heels together as you move.
- Keep your belly button in line with your opponent's (this way you will always be in front of her).

One of the best things about basketball is that even practice can be fun. Following are some fun games you can play that will help improve your defense.

Great defense can stop the other team from shooting baskets. Here, Cierra Burdick (#11) of the Tennessee Lady Vols defends against Sunny Greinacher (#14) of the Gonzaga Bulldogs.

Slide, Slide, Slide

Practice your defensive slides up and down the court against your partner, who can practice her dribbling at the same time. Three dribbles left, then three to the right. With each change of direction, you will open up your body to the defender, keeping your belly buttons in line, with your leg dropping back and sliding along with her. Switch roles and repeat this drill.

Simone Says

One player stands in front of at least two other players. She points in different directions. When she says, "Simone says slide right!" you do defensive slides to the right side of the court until "Simone says slide left!" (or "forward" or "backward"). You are out of the game if you stop or change directions when Simone did not tell you to. To trick you, Simone might point one way without saying "Simone says." Each player takes her turn as Simone.

Defense is a team game and help defense—where you move to guard another player or area if your teammate is having trouble containing her player—is key to good team defense. Also, taking a charge—planting your feet in front of a driving player and falling backward on your butt when she runs into you—will give your team possession of the ball and the other team a turnover and team foul. Players that play good help defense and take charges are most valuable to their team.

PASSING

Reasons you should make a pass include moving the ball up the court, involving teammates, and moving the defense. There are four main types of passes: chest pass, bounce pass, overhead pass, and baseball pass. The three skills to remember for passing are:

- Step toward your target.
- Aim at your target's chest.
- End with your arms out and thumbs toward the ground.

The chest pass is the quickest pass and goes directly from one player's chest to another's. The bounce pass skips off the ground two-thirds of the way between the passer and her target. Overhead passes travel long distances and work best when you want to pass to a teammate downcourt or on the opposite side of the court.

Following are some passing games to get you started. Whenever you pass, be sure your target is watching, and use fakes—make a move to pass one way and then quickly pass in another direction—so that the defense does not steal the ball.

Wall/Partner Pass

Practice passing the ball against a wall, or to a partner with the two of you 10 feet (3.05 m) apart: ten chest, ten bounce, ten overhead,

Diana Taurasi (#3) of the Phoenix Mercury prepares to pass the ball between two opponents from the Chicago Sky during a game of the WNBA Finals.

and ten baseball passes. You can use a wall for this; just remember to aim for a chest-high target.

Pass and Shoot

Cut out from the block to the wing and receive a chest pass from your partner who is at the top of the key. Turn and square up to the basket and shoot. Repeat ten times, then switch. Practice from both the right and left sides.

Try to pass and shoot from the post, as well. As you post up on the block and your partner passes to you from the wing, make a move and shoot. Passes into the post should be bounce passes. Remember to attempt to use fakes for all passes.

Keep Away

You need three players for this game. Also known as defense in the middle, it lets you work on your ball fakes and your defense. Stand 10 to 15 feet (3.05 to 4.57 m) away from another player, facing each other, with a defensive player in between the two of you. You have the ball and the defender is guarding you. You have to pass the ball to your partner without dribbling or moving and without the ball being stolen by the defender. The defender switches to the other player to play defense once you have passed her the ball. Rotate positions either when the defense gets a touch or after ten passes.

Remember, no matter how excellent one team member's handling of the ball is, passing is essential to keep the game going. Even the best player can be trumped by good defense. She'll need to send the ball to another player to advance toward the goal: scoring.

CHAPTER FOUR

SHOOTING AND REBOUNDING

Now that we've covered the basics of ball handling and moving across the court—as well as preventing the other team from doing so with solid defense—we can get into what happens when a player does make it to the hoop. In basketball, shooting is where the action's at! After all, it's how a team scores points. Equally important is knowing what to do when the ball bounces off the backboard from a missed shot. Let's cover shooting and rebounding.

SHOOTING

A consistent shooter—one who can make shots with either hand, under pressure, and from all over the court—is valuable to any team. The more you practice shooting, the better you'll get at it. Here are three basic tips for improving your shots:

- Stance: Your feet should be shoulder-width apart, with your shooting foot ahead of the other foot, your toes pointed toward the basket, and your knees bent.
- Form: Pull your elbows in at your sides. Make a backward C with your shooting arm with your wrist back (as if you were holding a tray). Put the ball on your finger pads. Your other arm is the guide hand and is not used to shoot.
- Follow-through: Extend your arm straight up; snap your wrist toward the basket.

Here are four fun games you can play to practice your hand at shooting.

Snap It

Start with ten shots up in the air. Then try ten with your opposite hand. This will be difficult at first, but the more you practice the stronger your muscles will get, and the easier it will be to shoot with either hand.

Around the World

Shoot from six different spots around the court, starting on one baseline, moving to the wing, the elbow, the other elbow, the other wing, and ending at the opposite baseline. Make two consecutive shots from each spot. Complete the entire trip across the court and back to make it "around the world."

Bank Shots

A bank shot is made by using the backboard to make a shot. Try this: From the box, and using only your shooting hand (no guide

Kristi Toliver of the University of Maryland's NCAA women's basketball team shoots the ball at a 2009 tournament practice. In 2010, Toliver joined the WNBA's Los Angeles Sparks.

hand), shoot until you make three out of five shots. Repeat, adding your guide hand. Then switch to the other block; repeat.

DRILLS FOR FOOTWORK AND WEIGHTLIFTING

In addition to all the skills we've outlined as the basics of basketball, agile footwork is also fundamental. Good footwork will help all areas of your game. Work on your speed, flexibility, and agility in each practice session. Skillful footwork isn't specific to basketball. Footwork drills will help with strength and agility in any sport. They should be performed three times a week.

Plyometrics is a type of jump training great for improving foot skills and building strength. Try hopping back and forth over a line with your left, right, and both feet. Do this first for twenty seconds each, then for thirty seconds each. Another good footwork training activity is box jumps. Set up a sturdy wooden box, or use a bench. Jump up and down from the box, landing softly each time. Repeat ten times.

Weightlifting is another activity you can do to build your strength for basketball. Basketball is a physical sport, with a good amount of pushing and muscling for position. Talk to your doctor and coach before starting with weights. Determine the right routine for your body and the game.

Layup Shots

Layups are shots taken on the move toward the basket. The technique used is different from any other shot in the game. From either side of the basket, dribble until you are two steps from the rim. Pick up your dribble and continue one and a half steps while holding the ball. From the right side, step first with your right foot, then with your left, and shoot with your right hand as your knee comes up. Reverse this when you shoot layups from the left side. Because layups often happen when you are going full-speed, on a fast break, or through defenders, practice different possible game situations.

REBOUNDING

A rebound is when a player grabs the ball after it bounces off of the rim or backboard on a missed shot. Rebounds are a very important part of basketball. When the defense rebounds, they get possession of the ball and the other team does not score. When the offense rebounds, they get another chance to score, usually from right under the basket.

You want to grab every missed shot you can get. The good news is that although you do usually have to jump for rebounds, you do not have to be the highest jumper to be a great rebounder. Here are three skills that are helpful to remember:

- Box out your player: Find a player on the other team (usually the player you are guarding), turn around, and make contact with your butt against their legs. Sit down into their legs.
- Jump to get the ball: When the ball bounces out into the court, go toward it and grab the rebound.
- Keep the ball above your chest, elbows out.

Here are some rebounding games to try.

Two players for the Washington Mystics try to take possession of the ball after a rebound, while three opponents from the Atlanta Dream try to stop them.

Toss It

Toss the ball high against a wall. Jump to catch it. Repeat. Once you get used to grabbing the ball off the bounce, add in an outlet pass. Keeping the ball above your head after the rebound, pivot toward the wing and pass to an outlet player using an overhead pass.

Wonder Woman

Stand on one block facing the basket. Throw the ball to the other side of the basket by bouncing it against the middle of the backboard. Slide over to the other side of the box, then jump and rebound the ball. Then throw the ball to the other side of the basket by bouncing it off the middle of the backboard again. Slide back and catch it. Repeat for fifteen to thirty seconds.

Jump Ball

You will need two friends for this game. One player tosses the ball up in the air in the middle of the other two (not too high). The other two try to box each other out and grab the rebound out of the air. Repeat ten times and then change spots. Each player takes her turn tossing the ball.

Once you've mastered shooting and rebounding, you're ready to win the game. The skills we've discussed—ball handling, passing, defense, shooting, and rebounding—are all a team needs to play competitively and win the game. Not everybody necessarily needs to be the best at each skill. That's what teammates are for! By working together and using your strengths, you can make the game fun and involved for every girl on the court.

CHAPTER FIVE

ALL NET: WOMEN'S COLLEGE BASKETBALL

Basketball isn't just a great way to make friends and stay healthy. It can also be an excellent path to college and, for the most talented players, a career. Basketball is one of the most successful college-level sports for women. In the 2013–14 season, the NCAA noted record-high numbers of teams across all three of its women's basketball divisions. It also publishes an important guide for high school students considering pursuing basketball in college (including academic standards such as a minimum GPA of 2.3). However, those lucky girls who catch the eye of the college scout may have access to scholarships and other resources to help pay for college.

So think about it. What do you want to accomplish in the next year? Do you want to make the varsity team? Lead your team in rebounding? Perfect your defense? Set goals that are both realistic and challenging, and keep your eyes on the rewarding prize: a college education.

THE PATH TO COLLEGE BASKETBALL

If you decide that you want to pursue basketball beyond high school, start planning by your junior year of high school. Research scholarships that are available for basketball players. Each year, the NCAA publishes an updated Guide for the College Bound Student Athlete. Ask your school's guidance counselor for a copy or find a digital version on the NCAA website. It will outline the steps you need to take to become active in college basketball.

There are many colleges that offer basketball programs even if you do not get a scholarship. Research the schools that interest you the most and contact the coaching staff. You will then want to ask your own coach if she or he can help you put together a video that highlights your skills. Your parents may be able to help with this as well.

All basketball players in middle school, high school, and college are student athletes. Remember that you are always a student first

SCHOLARSHIP SEARCH

Looking for the right scholarships can be daunting. Even if you find the right one, the paperwork may seem overwhelming. But don't despair! If you play high school basketball, there's likely a whole team of people invested in your future. Parents, coaches, and guidance counselors can all assist you in collecting the paperwork you need and filling out

(continued on the next page)

(continued from the previous page)

application forms. Coaches in particular can help you document your skills on the court with videos. Guidance counselors can help you collect progress reports and letters of recommendation from teachers and coaches. Your parents or an older sibling can proofread your submission letter.

There are also organizations that can help you get recruited. Founded in 2000, the National Collegiate Scouting Association (NCSA) is one of the largest organizations in the United States dedicated to helping student athletes navigate college recruiting. Since its founding, the NCSA has helped over sixty thousand student athletes receive over four billion dollars in scholarships. Search for the women's basketball scholarships that may be available for you at http://www.ncsasports.org /athletic-scholarships/womens-basketball.

The College Board is also a helpful organization for any student—basketball player or not—in the quest for scholarships and the right university. Its directory lists over two thousand colleges with women's basketball teams. By using the College Board's resources, any girl who plays basketball can learn what steps to take to get into college. It can even help you find a school that will waive your college application fee. Visit https://bigfuture .collegeboard.org to start looking for the right college for you.

If you might be interested in playing college basketball, your high school basketball coach or gym teacher can help guide you and give you the right advice.

and that you need to keep learning and working toward gradua-tion. You can never be sure when your basketball career might end because of an injury, burnout, or just a desire to try something new. Getting a good, well-rounded education will allow you to keep your options open. Furthermore, no matter how great of a basketball player a girl may be, no college will accept her with subpar academics.

If you receive a scholarship and then decide when you get to school that it is too much of a commitment—basketball occupies a good chunk of time each week for committed players—have a talk with the coaches and perhaps your academic advisor. There may be alternative scholar-ship opportunities or financial aid available to help you out. Don't feel trapped or helpless. There are always advisors to help you out.

Remember that as important as sports are, colleges always want a well-rounded individual. Keep academics a priority, and put in time studying and keeping up on homework!

MAKE IT HAPPEN!

Whatever level of basketball you choose to pursue, you're sure to learn highly valued skills. Your dedication to the sport, training both on and off the court, and the sense of teamwork you'll encounter will all teach you important life skills that will help you succeed in anything you pursue. The strength of character that it takes to step up and dedicate yourself to a team and a sport is invaluable. And you'll carry that with you each and every day, long after the final buzzer of your last game sounds. So don't hold back. Get involved in basketball and take advantage of all the opportunities that girls like you have in the world of athletics.

1891 James Naismith invents the game of basketball.

1893 Senda Berenson adapts the rules of basketball for women and introduces the game at Smith College.

1895 Clara Baer publishes the first rules adapted for women.

1899 Formation of the Women's Basketball Rules Committee.

1901 Spalding's Athletic Library publishes the first official guidebook on basketball for women.

1923 The Women's Division of the National Amateur Athletic Federation (NAAF) is formed.

1926 Amateur Athletic Union (AAU) sponsors the first-ever national women's basketball championship.

1928 The American Physical Education Association's (APEA) Section on Women's Athletics (SWA) forms the Women's National Officials Rating Committee (WNORC).

1955 The U.S. women's basketball team plays in the first Pan American Games women's basketball competition and wins the gold medal.

1969 The first Women's National Invitational Tournament, a collegiate women's basketball tournament, is held.

1976 A women's event in basketball makes its debut at the 1976 Summer Olympics held in Montreal, Canada. The Soviet Union wins the gold medal.

1978 The Women's Professional Basketball League is formed with eight teams. It lasts three seasons, until 1981.

1978 Carol Blazejowski is named the first recipient of the Wade Trophy, an award presented each year to the best player in NCAA Women's Basketball Division I competition.

1981 The Women's Basketball Coaches Association (WBCA) is formed.

1982 The first NCAA National Championship is held.

1984 Team USA captures its first Olympic gold medal in women's basketball in Los Angeles.

1988 Team USA wins the gold medal in women's basketball at the Seoul Olympics.

1991 Another attempt at a women's league occurs with the launch of the Liberty Basketball Association. However, the league folds after one game.

1992 Team USA wins the bronze medal at the Barcelona Olympics.

1992 The Women's Basketball Association is formed and lasts three seasons, until 1995.

1995 NCAA women's tournament expands from forty-eight teams to sixty-four, equal to that of the men's national tournament.

1996 Team USA recaptures the gold medal in women's basketball at the Centennial Olympics in Atlanta.

1997 The Women's National Basketball Association (WNBA) plays its inaugural season.

1999 The Women's Basketball Hall of Fame in Knoxville, Tennessee, holds its grand opening.

2000 Team USA wins the gold medal at the Sydney Olympics.

2003 The twenty-fifth anniversary of the first professional women's basketball game is celebrated.

2004 Team USA wins the gold medal at the Athens Olympics.

2008 Team USA wins the gold medal at the Beijing Olympics.

2012 Team USA wins the gold medal at the London Olympics.

2014 The WNBA Finals average 659,000 viewers across all ESPN channels, the highest viewership on record.

GLOSSARY

BOX OUT When a shot goes up and a defensive player keeps her opponent behind her back by sitting back into her legs and then jumping forward for the rebound. Critical for getting rebounds.

CHARGE When a defensive player plants her feet in front of an offensive player who then knocks her down, usually while driving to the basket. This is an offensive foul and results in possession for the defensive team.

DEFENSIVE STANCE Posture in which a defender bends her knees, with her back straight, playing low to the ground. This allows for quick moves and change of directions as she tries to prevent the offensive player from scoring or passing.

FLAGRANT FOUL Also known as an intentional foul, this is when a foul is committed on purpose such as grabbing a player around the waist. Usually an intentional foul is called when a player goes after another player's body, not the ball. The offensive player gets two free throws and then her team gets the ball out-of-bounds at half court.

FOLLOW-THROUGH The last motion at the end of a shot. The follow-through gives the ball its backward spin and makes it more likely to go in the basket.

FOUL Violation of the rules, signaled when a referee blows his or her whistle. Each player is allowed five fouls per game, six in the professional leagues.

FREE THROW A shot from the horizontal line at the top of the box taken after a player is fouled in the act of shooting. Each free throw earns one point.

HELP DEFENSE When a player leaves her area or assigned player and plays defense on another player in order to help her team.

OUTLET PASS Pass out from the key after a defensive rebound. Usually an overhead pass from a post player to a guard.

POINT GUARD The player who dribbles the ball up the court and calls the plays.

POST UP When a player turns her back to the basket, usually on the block, keeps her defender on her back by bending her knees and sitting back into the defense, and holds her hands up for an entry pass.

REBOUND When the offense or defense grabs a missed shot after it bounces off the rim and/or backboard.

SCREEN When an offensive player blocks a defender in order to get her teammate open. The screener must stand still on a screen, or else it is illegal and results in a turnover. Also referred to as "pick."

SHOOTING GUARD Also known as the two-guard, this player is usually a strong defender and has a good outside shot.

STEAL When a defender takes the ball away from the offense, usually by stealing a pass or knocking away a dribble.

SUBSTITUTION When a player from the bench comes on to the court to replace a teammate. Players can come in and out of games an unlimited number of times.

TECHNICAL FOUL A foul assessed for any of the following violations: delay of game, too many time-outs, too many players on the court, hanging on the rim, fighting, swearing, arguing with a referee, or being a poor sport. It results in one or two free throws and the ball out-of-bounds for the other team.

THREE-POINTER A successful shot made beyond the arc. In high school basketball, the semicircle is 19.75 feet (6.02 m) from the basket from all directions. College and professional leagues play with a longer three-point line.

TIME-OUT A break from the action. The coach or any player on the court can call a time-out.

TRAVELING When a player moves with the ball without dribbling. Also called walking.

TURNOVER When the team on offense loses possession of the ball in any way other than a missed shot.

FOR MORE INFORMATION

Canada Basketball
1 Westside Drive, Suite 11
Etobicoke, ON M9C 1B2
Canada
(416) 614-8037
Website: http://www.basketball.ca
Canada Basketball is the official national sporting organization
that regulates basketball in Canada. In addition to providing
leadership training, its Steve Nash Youth Basketball grass-
roots initiative promotes basketball among young adults and
children.

Canadian Association for the Advancement of Women and
Sport and Physical Activity (CAAWS)
N202 - 801 King Edward Avenue
Ottawa, ON K1N 6N5
Canada
(613) 562-5667
Website: http://caaws.ca
CAAWS provides leadership and education, and fosters equi-
table support, diverse opportunities, and positive
experiences for girls and women in sports.

Images of Us (IOU) Sports
1531 West Vliet Street
Milwaukee, WI 53205
(414) 934-0773

Website: http://www.iousports.org

IOU Sports provides sports education, fitness opportunities, and charitable assistance to girls who participate in all levels of sports. The organization's goal is to empower women using sports to teach discipline, teamwork, and fitness.

National Collegiate Athletic Association (NCAA)

700 West Washington Street

P.O. Box 6222

Indianapolis, IN 46206

(317) 917-6222

Website: http://www.ncaa.org/sports/womens-basketball

The NCAA regulates college-level sports throughout the United States, accounting for over 350 higher-level learning institutions and 170,000 student-athletes. Among the sports it regulates is women's college basketball.

National Council of Youth Sports (NCYS)

7185 Southeast Seagate Lane

Stuart, FL 34997

(772) 781-1452

Website: http://www.ncys.org

NCYS advocates the promotion of healthy lifestyles and safe environments for stronger neighborhoods and communities while enhancing the youth sports experience.

SHAPE America

1900 Association Drive

Reston, VA 20191

(800) 213-7193

Website: http://www.shapeamerica.org

Founded in 1885, SHAPE America is the largest network of educators and professionals involved in teaching and promoting physical education in the United States. It provides professional development to educators, as well as grants and scholarships to schools and students who promote and exhibit excellence in physical education and sports.

Women's Basketball Hall of Fame
700 Hall of Fame Drive
Knoxville, TN 37915
(865) 633-9000
Website: http://www.wbhof.com
Opened in 1999, the Women's Basketball Hall of Fame seeks to preserve and share the history of women's basketball, as well as memorialize women legends of the sport.

Women's National Basketball Association (WNBA)
645 Fifth Avenue
New York, NY 10022
(212) 688-9622
Website: http://www.wnba.com
Established in 1996, the WNBA is the women's counterpart to the National Basketball Association. It regulates professional women's basketball in the United States.

Women's Sports Foundation
247 West 30th Street, Suite 7R
New York, NY 10001
(646) 845-0273
(800) 227-3988
Website: http://www.womenssportsfoundation.org

Since 1974, the Women's Sports Foundation has dedicated
    itself to advancing the lives of girls and women through
    sports and physical activity.

WomenSport International (WSI)
P.O. Box 743
Vashon, WA 98070
Website: http://www.sportsbiz.bz/womensportinternational/
    index.htm
WSI works to promote the values of physical activity in the lives
    of young women and to bring about positive change for
    women in sports.

YWCA USA
2025 M Street NW, Suite 550
Washington, DC 20036
(202) 467-0801
Website: http://www.ywca.org
The YWCA seeks to eliminate racism and empower women
    through sports and other community activities at over 1,300
    locations nationwide.

WEBSITES

Because of the changing nature of Internet links, Rosen
Publishing has developed an online list of websites related to
the subject of this book. This site is updated regularly. Please
use this link to access the list:

http://www.rosenlinks.com/IX/Basket

FOR FURTHER READING

Allen, Kathy. *Girls Race! Amazing Tales of Women in Sports*. North Mankato, MN: Capstone Press, 2014.

Augustyn, Adam, ed. *The Britannica Guide to Basketball*. New York, NY: Britannica Educational Publishing, 2011.

Bekkering, Annalise. *NCAA Basketball*. New York, NY: AV2 by Weigl, 2014.

Bryant, Jill. *Women Athletes Who Changed the World*. New York, NY: Rosen Publishing, 2012.

Campbell, Forest G., and Fred Ramen. *An Insider's Guide to Basketball*. New York, NY: Rosen Central, 2015.

Doeden, Matt. *All About Basketball*. North Mankato, MN: Capstone Press, 2015.

Finch, Jennie. *Throw Like a Girl: How to Dream Big and Believe in Yourself*. Chicago, IL: Triumph Books, 2011.

Grange, Michael, and Wayne Embry. *Basketball's Greatest Stars*. 3rd ed. Richmond Hill, ON: Firefly Books, 2015.

Howell, Brian. *Cheryl Miller: Basketball Hall of Famer & Broadcaster*. Minneapolis, MN: ABDO Publishing, 2014.

Krause, Jerry, Don Meyer, and Jerry Meyer. *Basketball Skills & Drills*. 3rd ed. Champaign, IL: Human Kinetics, 2008.

La Bella, Laura. *Women and Sports*. New York, NY: Rosen Publishing, 2013.

Miller, Karen. *Girls and Sports*. Detroit, MI: Greenhaven Press, 2010.

Omoth, Tyler. *The Ultimate Collection of Pro Basketball Records*. North Mankato, MN: Capstone Press, 2013.

Phelps, Richard. *Basketball for Dummies*. 3rd ed. Hoboken, NJ: Wiley, 2011.

Rappoport, Ken. *Ladies First: Women Athletes Who Made a Difference*. Atlanta, GA: Peachtree Publishers, 2010.

Ross, Betsy M. *Playing Ball with the Boys: The Rise of Women in the World of Men's Sports*. Cincinnati, OH: Clerisy Press, 2010.

Samuels, Mina. *Run Like a Girl: How Strong Women Make Happy Lives*. New York, NY: Seal Press, 2011.

Schweitzer, Karen. *Sheryl Swoopes*. Broomall, PA: Mason Crest, 2013.

Storm, Hannah. *Go Girl! Raising Healthy, Confident, and Successful Girls Through Sports*. Chicago, IL: Sourcebooks, 2011.

Stout, Glenn. *Yes, She Can! Women's Sports Pioneers*. New York, NY: Sandpiper, 2011.

Ware, Susan. *Game, Set, Match: Billie Jean King and the Revolution in Women's Sports*. Chapel Hill, NC: University of North Carolina Press, 2011.

Whitaker, Matthew C. *African American Icons of Sport: Triumph, Courage, and Excellence*. Boston, MA: Greenwood Press, 2008.

Williams, Doug. *Girls' Basketball*. North Mankato, MN: ABDO Publishing, 2014.

Winters, Jaime. *Center Court: The History of Basketball*. New York, NY: Crabtree Publishing, 2016.

INDEX

ABOUT THE AUTHORS

Barry Mableton is an outdoors lover and big-time sports fan. He lives in Castleton-on-Hudson in upstate New York.

Elizabeth Gettelman is a journalist and sports equity specialist who lives in San Francisco, California. She is also active in getting girls involved in sports.

PHOTO CREDITS